Grow Your Business

Proven Marketing Tips to Grow Your Business and the Use of Social Media

By

Joe Leo

ISBN-13-978-1499259476

ISBN-10-1499259476

Table Of Contents

Introduction

Several years ago I was interviewing for a marketing directors position with a medical supply company that had multiple locations. During the interview the president of the company said that he decided to look for a marketing person because he just couldn't come up with any new fresh ideas for his ads. I knew I was in trouble right off the bat, because I now knew that he was confusing advertising with marketing. The question that kept racing through my mind was how do I tell the president of this company that he was looking at marketing the wrong way?

You see while advertising is an important part of the marketing mix it is only one small part of the big picture. Marketing a business for growth involves a number of factors and it has to be not only consistent, but also comprehensive and customized to the target market of the business.

The president of the company proceeded to ask me all the typical interview questions about my background, my experience and my education and then he told me a lot about his company. After about an hour into the interview process, he sat back in his chair, looked me straight in the eye and said "Well what do you think?" ..."Do you think you have what it takes to develop new ads for this company and help us grow this business?"

I sat back in my chair mirroring his move and said "Yes I know I can help you grow this business, but I think that we need to look at the whole picture and utilize a variety of marketing techniques .... and not just ads" I could tell from the puzzled look on his face that he wasn't really sure what I was talking about .... so I continued. I began telling him that advertising is just a small part of marketing and that there are a lot of other things that we could do to grow the business. He leaned forward in his chair and said ... "What kind of things?" Now I had his attention, so I leaned forward in my chair, again mirroring his moves and I said well … first we need to develop a marketing plan and identify who your target market really is, then we need to identify who we are and what this companies unique marketing statement is going to be. We need to figure out why your products and services are better than your competition and then we need to develop a marketing budget to outline how much we are willing to spend on marketing and then we need to ….and before I could get another word out of my mouth … he stood up and said … "OK … the job is yours … when can we get started?"

I didn't realize it at the time but that was the day that the outline for this book actually started. Over the next 25+ years working in marketing for a variety of companies, owning several of my own businesses and doing consulting work I compiled the proven marketing techniques outlined in this book.

When I sat down to write this book I had the small and medium businesses in mind, but these techniques can be utilized by any size company that is looking to grow their business. Small to medium sized businesses usually require the most help when it comes to marketing. The reason being, that these businesses are usually started by someone that has a passion for what they are doing. However, even though they are great at what they do in most cases they have always worked for somebody else and never owned their own business and as a result they really don't have any marketing experience.

Most large companies can afford to either hire a marketing consulting firm or hire employees to develop a marketing department. If you are reading this book and you are from one of those large companies that has hired a marketing company or started your own marketing department … I challenge you to read this book and make sure that all of the techniques in this book are being utilized by the people you have entrusted with the responsibility of doing the marketing for your company!

After reading this book and applying these marketing tips to your business … you will "Grow Your Business" and increase your bottom line.

Chapter 1

The Marketing Plan

"If you fail to plan, you are planning to fail"

Benjamin Franklin

Every successful business has a marketing plan. It doesn't have to be complex, it can be as little as one sheet of paper but it must answer a few key questions.

1. Where are we right now?
2. What products do we sell or what service do we provide?
3. Who is our target market?
4. Why are we different from our competition?
5. What is our unique selling proposition?
6. What is our marketing goal?
7. How much money do we have for marketing?

Write down the answers to all these questions … yes write them down; don't just keep the answers in your mind. Why do I have to write it down you ask? Because you need to be able to look back at your answers on a regular basis and make sure that the answers have not changed and that you are still on track.

Ok let's get started: #1 Where are we right now? – What is your company's current situation? Are you making money or are you losing money? What are our annual sales for the current year? Did we improve over last year? How were our sales over the last 3 or 5 years? What are we doing differently now than we did when we first started the company? How many customers do we have? How many of those customers are repeat customers? How did we get the customers we have?

#2 What products do we sell or what services do we provide? – Make a list of your products or services. Have we added or deleted any over the past year, 3 years, 5 years? Has adding or deleting any of our products or services impacted our business growth? What products or services can we add or delete over the next year to improve our bottom line? What products or services can we add to attract additional customers from various demographic groups?

#3 Who is our target market? – Is it men, women, children or all of them? What is the average age of our customers? Where are our customers coming from? Are They within a 5 mile radius or a 10 mile radius from our business? Are they coming from across town or from the next state? What are the demographics of our customers (salary range, ethnic background etc.)? How can we get more customers from the customers we already have?

#4 Why are we different from our competition? – Why do our customers purchase our products and services instead of our competitors? What do we do differently than they do? What are our strengths? What are our weaknesses? How is our pricing compared to theirs?

#5 What is our unique selling proposition? – Or - What is our unique Marketing statement? What sets us apart from our competitors? How do we want people to remember us?

#6 What is our marketing goal? – Do we want to add new products and services over the next year, two years and five years? What is a realistic growth for our company over the next year, two years and 5 years … is it 10%, 20% or more? Do we want to attract other demographic groups?

#7 How much money do we have for marketing? How much did we spend last year? How much did we spend in previous years?

How does what we spent compare to our growth in those years? Most small to medium sized companies allocate about 10% of their annual gross sales to marketing, but there are many businesses that only allocate 2-5% of their gross sales. You be the judge here and start out with whatever is comfortable for you and your business. Remember, that not all of the marketing techniques in this book are going to cost you money. Many great marketing strategies can be accomplished with little or no money.

Now that you have the answers to all these questions we can actually take action toward your goals. Remember none of your answers are cast in stone and your marketing plan should be revisited every month or quarter to see if you are on track and if you need to re-evaluate some of your answers. Business environments change and so do the consumers buying habits, so it's a good idea to revisit your plan and make changes as necessary.

Chapter 2

The Marketing Budget

In Chapter 1 – Question #6 we discussed how much money do we have for marketing. If you answered all the questions then you should have a dollar amount in mind. Now we need to take that number and develop a budget. Once again this is not cast in stone, because as you go through the year you might find that one of the marketing strategies is working better than the other and in that case you can move your money around within the budget.

Here is a sample budget that I used for one of the companies that I did work for.

Total Marketing Budget Amount	**$35,000**
Newspaper ads	$ 3,000
Printing	$ 5,000
Radio Ads	$15,000
Website Development	$ 900
Social Media	$ 1,500
Advertising Specialties	$ 8,000
Community Events	$ 1,000
Donations	$ 600
Total	**$35,000**

Now don't get scared. I am not trying to tell you that you need to allocate $35,000 to marketing. This was just simply an illustration of one company that I worked for. When I started working with this company they had no advertising budget and they weren't doing very much marketing. The company was doing gross sales in excess of $1.2 million dollars and they had been stagnant for a few years with very little to no growth. When I proposed this marketing budget, which by the way was very conservative, it conjured up quite a conversation at the board meeting. In the end however they approved my proposed budget and at the end of the first year the company grew about 15% in gross sales. The following year I asked for an increase in the budget and I got my increase every year from the board of directors without any argument. Why? Because I showed them how it worked and I showed them the ROI (return on investment) by boosting their bottom line. I also tracked all of the marketing techniques that I used that first year and showed them how each area contributed to the 15% growth.

Small business owners today cited customer attraction and retention as two of their most pressing concerns, but many of them set aside minimal budgets for marketing. In fact 1 in 4 small business owners reported that they don't spend any money on marketing, while just over half (56%) spend less than $500 a month. This means that only about a quarter of business owners spend more than $500 per month on marketing. In August 2013 Yodle (yodle.com local online advertising experts) conducted their first annual small business survey and the results were shocking. 23% of the businesses spent nothing on marketing, 38% spent between $1.00 - $249 a month, 18% spent between $250 - $499 per month, 10% spent $500 - $749 per month, 3% spent $750 - $999 per month, 6% spent $1,000 - $2,000 per month and 3% spent over $2,000 per month.

My point is that this should be the year that you allocate a larger more flexible budget to take advantage of new marketing opportunities. Once again I am not saying that you should break the bank, but I want you to make strategic investments in marketing programs that will improve the position of your business in places where your target market goes to research products and services.

There is no doubt in my mind that businesses that stay stagnant and continue to utilize minimal marketing in today's rapidly changing environment will only hurt their bottom line.

One of my college professors said 50% of most marketing campaigns don't work and 50% of the campaigns work great. Your job is to figure out what is working and do more of that and eliminate what is not working. He then gave us an in depth lesson on marketing analytics and how to track our results to achieve the most ROI. The best way to track your ROI (return on investment) is to first know where you are right now before you started using the marketing techniques in this book. Figure out how many customers you have right now, how much are they currently spending, and what are your total gross sales by month, and by the quarter.

This will be your baseline before marketing. Now you can compare this years results by month, quarter and the year using the same parameters. How many customers did we have before we started marketing vs. How many customers do we have now? How much did these customers spend before we started marketing vs. how much are they spending now? And finally …. What were our gross sales by month and by the quarter before we started marketing vs. what are our current sales now by the month and by the quarter?

This is a very simple way to measure your growth and to see if your marketing is working. You might find that current customers are spending more as a result of your marketing because you are now sending out email coupons or announcing special events. You might find that you grew your customer base by adding 100 new customers over the last 6 months. You might also see that sales went up 10% in the first quarter of this year as compared to last year. This is when you go back and review your marketing plan to see what it was that you were doing during that time that could have caused that increase.

If this is your first year in business simply compare the first month to the next month and then the next month etc. until you establish that first years baseline. However if you are consistently following the tips in this book you should see an increase in customers and sales from month to month during your first year. If you don't then you need to add in some new techniques to the ones that you have already implemented until you see the business start to grow.

Chapter 3

What Is Marketing?

What is marketing? The dictionary describes marketing as *"the action or business of promoting and selling products or services, including market research and advertising"*

BusinessDictionary.com describes marketing as *"The management process through which goods and services move from concept to the customer. It includes the coordination of four elements called the 4 P's of marketing:"*

1. Identification, selection and development of a **Product**.

2. Determination of **Price**.

3. Selection of a distribution channel to reach the customers **Place**.

4. Development and implementation of a **Promotional** strategy.

The fact of the matter is that in order to grow your business, you need to attract and retain a large base of satisfied customers. To do this you must determine the needs of your customers and analyze your competitive advantages to develop a marketing plan. You must also select specific markets to serve and determine how to satisfy your customers' needs by identifying and implementing a good marketing mix.

Most small businesses don't have unlimited amounts of capital that they can devote to marketing but you can still realize excellent returns if you focus on target marketing and concentrating your efforts on one or a few key market groups.

Some of the trends that affect sales and profitability are shifting populations, legal developments and the local economic situation. These trends should be monitored regularly so that you can quickly identify any problems or potential opportunities. It is also very important to keep an eye on your competitor's current marketing strategies.

Marketing also requires that everyone in your company who plays a role in satisfying the customers needs understand your marketing goals.

Marketing your business is an ongoing job so make sure that you actively engage in at least one marketing activity everyday. Make sure you have a marketing budget and that you have determined what percentage of your gross income you will be spending annually on marketing. Set specific marketing goals for the year and review them and adjust them quarterly. In addition always and I mean always carry business cards with you at all times because you never know who you are going to meet.

As I mentioned earlier in the introduction of this book marketing is more than just advertising. Although advertising is an important part of the mix its not the only thing a business should be doing if they want to grow. As the dictionary clearly state it's "the action or business of promoting and selling".

Ok… so your asking yourself … what else can I do to promote my business … relax and just keep reading, because I am about to unveil proven marketing techniques that **WILL** increase your bottom line and grow your business.

The following list is just an example of some of the proven marketing techniques, many of which we will cover in greater detail in the rest of this book.

1. Website (Content & SEO)

2. Facebook

3. Twitter and Linkedin

4. Branding Your Business

    a. Logos, taglines, business and vehicle signage, business cards, letterheads, brochures and employee uniforms.

5. Free Ads On Backpage and Craigslist

6. Email Marketing

    a. Newsletters, special promotions, new product announcements, coupons

7. Radio & Television Advertising

8. Direct Mail Advertising

    a. Postcards, Val-Pak Coupons

9. Print Advertising

    a. Newspapers, Placemats, Billboards, Fax Blasts, Door Hangers, Lawn Signs, Brochures, Community & School Ad Journals, Church & Synagogue Newsletters & Bulletins, Press Releases, & Business Profiles

10. Networking Events

11. Video Marketing (You Tube Channel)

12. Internal Marketing

    a. Customer referral programs, Open House, Special Events, Gift Certificates, Customer Surveys, Contests, Customer Relations, Thank You Cards

13. Speaking at local groups and organizations

14. Sponsoring Local Events

    a. Golf Outings, Charity Fund-Raising Walks

15. Chamber of Commerce Dinners & Networking Functions

16. Local web based directories

17. Marketing with non-competitive business neighbors

18. Community Organizations (Rotary, Lions, Elks etc.)

19. Cold Calling / Face To Face Interaction

20. Trade Shows, Health Fairs & Expos

    a. Advertising Specialties, Special Promotions, Contests & Drawings

I know … you are reading this list and your thinking I know about all of these … I thought you were going to tell me something new and exciting.

My answer to you is simply this … how many of these things have you actually tried and tried consistently? I will bet maybe one or two at the most and when you didn't see immediate results you gave up and said "This stuff doesn't work".

These 20 marketing techniques are proven tried and true ways to grow your business but you must do it with consistency and you must be targeting the right market for your business. Let me ask you a question. If you own a dog grooming business would you market your services to people that don't have any pets or people that have cats? The answer of course is NO … this is not your target market … you need to market to the people who own dogs.

If you owned a Radiology company and you offer Mammography services for women … who is your target market? The answer is women between the ages of 45-74. So you find where those people are and then you market your services to them.

Too many times businesses just market or advertise for the sake of getting their name out there and 50% or more of their marketing dollars are wasted on people that are not within their target market. Yes … 50% of your marketing is not working, so find out what isn't working and why it's not working. Pinpoint your target market and promote your business to them …. and you will grow your business!

Newspapers and Radio Stations know who their target market is and they can give you a breakdown of age, sex, income and demographic groups within the areas that they reach. Maybe you are running your ads in the wrong newspapers or on the wrong radio stations for your target market, because you never took the time to do the research.

Once you have implemented a marketing plan you must evaluate its performance. Every marketing plan should have performance standards that you can compare to the actual results.

A well organized, well defined marketing plan can do wonders for your company. It should at the least: remind customers and inform prospective customers about the benefits of your products or services. It will help you maintain a distinct identity and enhance you reputation as well as increase sales to boost your bottom line.

Chapter # 4

Your Company Website

You do have a company website … don't you?

If you don't have a company website … then stop reading right now, put this book down and go work on putting together a website.

If you can't afford to hire a website designer … then make one yourself at www.godaddy.com or at www.weebly.com these sites are excellent and will guide you through the set-up and design. They are both very user friendly even to a novice computer user. They both offer a variety of templates for different types of businesses and they both will guide you in also making your website mobile, so that it will be compatible to mobile devices like the Ipad, Iphone and other smart phones. This is very important because many people today use their hand held devices to search for products and services and if your website is not compatible to mobile devices it will be very hard for your prospective customer to navigate your website. Take a look at your competitions web sites and get some ideas and then get started. I am not a professional web designer and I have used both of these companies to help a few of my clients set up their websites. You can always transfer your domain name to a web site designer down the road and have your site re-done professionally when you have the money, but in most cases if you build it using one of the sites I mentioned above … this will not be necessary.

The important thing is to get a website up and get your name out there. The beauty about using one of these companies is that they also submit your site to all the major search engines and they host the site for you for as little as $50.00 per year, the last time I checked. When they submit your site to the search engines they do it with the use of keywords and this is what will get your name to pop up when somebody does a search. Lets say for example you are a painting contractor … some of the keywords you might use are: interior painting, exterior painting, custom painting, painter etc. Now when a person does a search on the computer for a painter in the area and they use one of those keywords in their search, your company name will appear on their search list, without them even knowing your company name.

Always make sure that your website is submitted correctly to all the major search engines, by checking on Google, Bing, Yelp, YP.com, and Superpages.com just to name a few. Sometimes not all of the information gets picked up correctly during submission … In fact a Constant Contact Survey done earlier this year found that 50% of small businesses had found inaccurate listings for their business. Despite this over 49% of these businesses said they never took the time to update their business listings online. WHY?? … this is important information that tells your customers a lot about your company and if the information is incorrect it gives people the impression that you don't care about your business.

Check your business listing and certify that your business is listed accurately using services like Localeze, Axiom, SinglePlatform, and Universal Business Listing since these are the primary listings providers for local websites.

Having a website for your company is so important today in order for people to find you. Remember the days of the old yellow page books? When somebody wanted a painter or an electrician … all they had to do was go to the yellow pages and look under the heading painters or electricians and there was a listing of people in the area. Well for the most part the yellow pages are a thing of the past. I know that there is a smaller version of the yellow pages called yellow book or something like that and from time to time you will find a copy of that book on your doorstep when you get home from work. A few months ago I found one on my doorstep and do you know what I did with it ? I picked it up and tossed it right in the garbage. What do I need it for? I can find anything that I need right on the internet and I can access it from my computer, my phone or my Ipad and that is what a large majority of people do today. That is why you must have a presence on the internet.

Ok ... now let's talk about the content of your website. This is important because once people find you; you want them to stay and look at what you have to offer and then pick up the phone and call you. The first page, which is your homepage, is your chance to grab their attention and tell them who you are, what you do, where you are located and how they can get in touch with you. So the homepage should contain your company logo (and don't tell me you don't have a logo of some kind ... but if you don't we will be talking about logos in the chapter about "Branding" later in this book). Now let's get back to your homepage, you need to have your company logo, company name, address, phone #, email address and your company tagline (oh no ... you don't have a tagline ... then get one now ... we will also be talking about this in the chapter on "Branding"). These six items need to be right there at the top of your homepage so as soon as somebody visits your website ... you just answered all of the questions they want answered. Who you are, where you are located and how can I get in touch with you.

The homepage should also have a brief bio and pictures about the company explaining what your company does. Pictures are important, because too much text looks boring and pictures capture the eye of the person looking at your site. The picture should be something that adds to your bio. If you, are the company, then put your picture up there with your name and title under the picture. If you're a painting company you might want to put a picture of your truck or a picture of a room you have painted, showing the quality of your work. That is all your homepage needs, anything else and it is too cluttered and people will not take the time to look at it. Now you want to start designing additional pages that are specific to what you do. For example if you are a painter, the next page might be called "Services Offered." Under this tab you would make a list of the products or services you provide. The next one might be "Photo Gallery" and on this page you can display pictures of your finished jobs or if you're a restaurant …. pictures of the inside of the restaurant or pictures of food. Your next page could be a "Contact Us" page, where once again you can list your name, address, phone #, Fax #, email address and other locations that you might have. You can also put a request form on this page, where people can answer specific questions and ask for information. Make sure on your request form that you ask for all the potential customers information (name, address, phone # and email address) not only so you can get back to them and provide the information that they requested but also to start building a customer database that you can use down the road, after I teach you about email marketing, newsletters, contests and coupons.

A number of other pages can be added to your website as needed to emphasize other areas of your business. One of my websites is for a group of entertainers. They have a page on their site that shows their current schedule, so that people can check in and see where they are performing. They also have a page where people can go to purchase their CD's or T-Shirts. This is also easy to set-up, just by following the instructions for setting up an online store. Most hosting sites will offer this option to you complete with credit card processing right through the site or with the use of a Paypal account. Another one of my customers who owns a pest control company has a page on his website with pictures of different insects and an explanation of where they come from, what attracts them to your property and how the pest control company treats your property to get rid of them.

One website page that is becoming very popular today is a page where people can go and view videos about your business. These videos can be as simple as photos set to music or as complex as a music video. People enjoy looking at these videos and they will stay and browse your site longer if it contains interesting content like photos and videos. You can even take this one step further by linking your video to You Tube where you can have your own video channel …. and it's free. Later in this book we will be talking about videos with instructions about linking videos to your website, Facebook and You Tube and how to set up your own You Tube channel.

Now your website is complete and you have a presence on the internet for everyone to see … oh but … they can't see your website unless they know your website address or if they do a search with keywords and you pop up in the search.

Your job now … is to drive traffic to your website and the best way to do that is to make sure that you use good keywords, so that people searching on line can find you.

The other way is to make sure your website address is included on all of your marketing materials (business cards, business signs, vehicle signs etc.). The more that people see your address, the more they will visit your site and the more they visit your site …. the higher your business will go up in the search ratings, without having to pay for premium spots.

One of the companies that I did work for took my advice and used their website address on everything that they did. They also linked their Facebook Page and Twitter Account as well as their Linkedin page back to their website. Within 30 days they went from #56 in a Google search (which meant their listing was on about the 7th or 8th page of the Google search) to the first page of the search in the #2 spot right under one of the paid sponsor ads.

We will talk more about linking your other on line marketing efforts with your website later on in this book when we discuss Facebook, Twitter and Linkedin and other Social Media.

Today's emphasis in the business environment is on ecommerce, rapid business transactions and the ability to quickly access information. This has changed consumer behavior as well as their expectations and your business must be actively involved in this social network if you want to survive.

My suggestion is to surf the web and look at a lot of different websites and make notes of what info they have on their websites. Look closely at the different types of pages that they have included on their website and you are sure to get plenty of ideas that will help you design or re-design your website.

Chapter # 5

Your Facebook Page

Your company must have a Facebook page, no question about it. It is easier to set up than a website and it will do a variety of things for your company. A Facebook page will allow you to have customers "Like" your page, see what is going on at your business and make comments about your products or services. It will give you a great way to announce new products and services, special events and to post articles and information pertinent to your type of business that will educate your customers. Every time you post something on Facebook, everybody that has "Liked" your page will see the information that you posted on their news feed. Getting the word out to these people and it cost you nothing but a little bit of time.

Here is how you set up a Facebook page if you have never done one for your company or if you don't have a personal Facebook page already. If you already have a personal page set-up the steps to set-up a business page are slightly different and we will cover them in Step #9.

1. Go to www.facebook.com

2. On the right side of the page you will see an area that says sign up and directly under that is a few boxes that you need to fill in with information. Once you complete that step and click on sign up it will take you to the next page.

3. This page will give you the opportunity to find friends that you might already know that are on Facebook, through Gmail, Outlook, Yahoo and other email accounts that you might have.

4. When you have completed that step or skipped that step it will take you to the next page that will ask you for some profile information (your hometown, schools etc.). You can complete this step or skip it at this point if you would like, because you can always fill in this information at a later time.

5. The next page is where they ask you to choose your interests, by clicking "Like" on any of the pictures and subjects it will send you information about them on your news feed when they post something. Once again you can either complete this step or you can skip it and do it a later time.

6. The next page is where they ask you to upload a profile picture. This is where you can put your own picture or a copy of the company logo or a picture of your building etc. You can either upload a picture you already have on your computer or you can take a picture with your webcam if your computer is equipped with one. Once again you have the opportunity to complete this step or skip it and come back to it later.

7. The next page says Welcome to Facebook. This just means that your basic info is ready to go and you will be able to start posting to your page shortly. On this page they will ask you again if you want to find friends by using your email address contact list. The next section will give you a tour about the privacy settings and explain each setting as to who can and can not see your postings. When it's a business page I always suggest that you use the public privacy setting. This means that every body can see your company's activity. I know some people that choose the friends setting, which only allows people that have liked the page to see their posts. This is entirely up to you. The final section of this page gives you the opportunity once again to "Like" any pages that you

might be interested in receiving information from in your news feed.

8. On the left side of this page you will see a list of functions that you can choose from. The first one at the very top should be your name and under that it will say edit profile. Then you will see links for welcome, news feed, messages etc. If you click on the name of your business it will take you to your page where you can start posting information. At the top right hand side of this page will be a green box that says take a tour. I highly suggest that you take the tour and learn all you can about how all the other options are used. To make your page official you must go to your email and find the email that they sent you. The email will ask you to confirm your email address and you can do this by simply clicking on that link. The email will also give you a code, copy the code down, just in case they ask you for it later when you sign in. Sometimes they ask for the code and sometimes they don't, so just be prepared in case they do. Some of the steps that I have outlined for you might change from the time this book is published and the time you try to set up your page, because Facebook is always making changes to improve their site and make it more user friendly, but don't fret it is simple and very self explanatory.

9. If you already have a personal Facebook page that you use to interact with your friends and family all you need to do is log-in to your page and look up at the top right hand side of the screen and you will see a few symbols. The first symbol is for finding friends or requesting friends. The second one is if you want to private message your friends or go back to look at old conversations that you might have had in the past. The third one is where you can see any notifications, game requests and comments that people have made on your page or about a picture or something you posted. The next symbol

looks like a lock and that is where you can set up your security settings. I would definitely take some time to look at this area, just so that you are familiar with how you can protect your privacy on Facebook. The last symbol looks like a downward arrow and if you click on that symbol a roll down window will open. In this roll down window you have a couple of choices but the only thing that we are going to talk about right now is the one that says Create Page. Click on this link and it will bring you to a page that gives you 6 types of business pages to choose from. The one that we are going to use today for illustration purposes is the first box that says Local Business or Place. This is specifically for a physical brick and mortar business such as a restaurant or a dry cleaner etc. If your business is not a brick and mortar location then you simply click on the next box which is called Company, Organization or Institution. There are also other choices for Artists and Bands and one for Entertainment as well as one for Causes and Community. Look at all of them and choose the one that best suits your business. They all work basically the same as the example that I am giving you. So once you click on the first box Local Business or Place another box is going to open. The first line will say Choose Your Category. Click on that box and a drop down window will open giving you a list of business types. Just click on the business that is closest to yours and that will appear in the top box. The rest is self explanatory … you need to fill in the name of your business, address, city, state, zip code and phone # and then click on the link at the bottom that says Get Started. Whatever name you enter for the business name is going to be the name of the page, so make sure you like the name, because it is almost impossible to change the name once you have established the page. Once you click on Get Started it is going to take you to another page and start asking for information about the business. Simply answer the questions and then click on Save Info. The next page will ask you to upload an image. Like I mentioned earlier this image can be your picture, a picture of the business, or a picture of your logo etc. The next page will instruct you to add this new page to your favorites list. This way a link will appear on the left hand side of your home page / news feed page and make it easy for you to access it whenever you want. Once you complete that step the next page will prompt you to create an ad for your business. If you're not ready to place an ad yet don't worry about it and just click on the button that says Skip. You can always create an ad at another time and we will be talking about ads later in this chapter. After you click on skip it will take you directly to your new page and all the info that you entered will be on that page. The rest is simple, just enter posts and post pictures about your business the same way you do it on your personal page.

Now you need to let everybody know that you have a Facebook page and ask them to take a look at your page and click the "Like" button. Some suggestions that I have to attract people to your page are as follows:

1. Put a Facebook link on your website, so that people can click on the link and it will take them directly to your page. Also make sure that you also put your website address on your Facebook page, so that people can link to your website directly from Facebook.

2. Put up a sign in your business that says "Like Us On Facebook" if you have the type of business that people come to visit. You can also print it on the back of your business cards or on any other marketing materials that you print.

3. You can also include your Facebook address along with your website address on all of your literature (business cards, brochures, print ads, invoices etc.)

4. If you already have a personal page and you followed my directions in #9 on how to set up a new page … your new page will show a list of all your friends from your personal page. On the right side of your page you will see a box called "Invite Friends". All you have to do is click on the button that says "Invite" next to each of your friends and they will be sent a message telling them that you have invited them to "Like" your new page.

5. You can also message your friends and give them a link to your new page and ask them to post it on their page and share it with their friends. This method works great … I have a friend who owns a restaurant that did this and within 24 hours he had over 300 "Likes" on his new page. Remember the more people that you can attract to your page the faster your business name will spread and the faster your business will grow.

6. Take out Facebook ads, which we will be talking about in a couple of minutes.

7. Link your Facebook page and your website with the other forms of social media that you are using (Twitter, Linkedin etc).

It is important to note that Facebook recently reported that over 24 million small businesses maintain active pages on their site!

Facebook Ads

Placing an ad on Facebook is easy and there are a couple of ways to do it. The best part is you get to set the budget of how much you want to spend per day or per campaign.

Looking at your page you will see a Blue Button on the top right side that says "Promote Page". Simply click on this button and complete the questions. A little further down the right side you will see another Blue Button and this one says "Boost Post". Simply click on that button and complete the questions. It's that simple!

Wait there is more …. You can also go to your home page / news feed page and on the left side you will see the words "Create An Ad", if you click on this it will open a page that gives you a choice of about 8 different types of ads each created to do something specific. If you hover over the links with your mouse it will explain exactly what that particular ad will do. When you find one that you like click on the link and it will open another page that will guide you through placing that ad. Like I said before, these ads allow you to set your budget so it is up to you how much money you want to spend.

Another great way to advertise a promotion on your Facebook page is to design an ad or special coupon just for your Facebook friends and include that ad or coupon as a picture (JPEG) as an attachment to one of your posts. One of the companies that I work with is a pest control company and at the end of the winter they placed a coupon in their Facebook post offering $200 off any termite treatment. This post of course was only seen by the people, who "Liked" their page, but it proved very successful and as a result several customers called to set up appointments. Marketing on Facebook is a great way to grow your business, all you need to do is be consistent and post everyday or at least three times a week to keep your name out in front   of your Facebook friends.

It is also important to note that just as I mentioned before ... traffic to your website will boost you in the search engines. The same goes for activity and postings on your Facebook page. One of my friends who owns a restaurant posted something on his Facebook page every day about the restaurant and when one of his customers did a search on the business ... the first thing that popped up in the search results in the #1 spot right below the paid sponsor ads was the restaurants name and a link to their Facebook page. His website also popped up in the search, but it was further down on the results page.

It's going to take a little bit of your time to do the things that I have outlined, but in the end it is going to pay-off. Don't get discouraged if nothing happens in the first week or the first month, just keep doing it ... be consistent and the results will amaze you.

Chapter 6

Twitter and Linkedin

Twitter and Linkedin are two great social media sites to also help promote and grow your business. I could actually devote an entire book to these to entities but in this book I will give you the basic information that you need to get started. If you are somewhat savvy at using the computer and the internet you will be able to navigate both of these sites in a very short time. If you are looking for additional information about how to use these sites beyond what I have given you here in this book, there are a number of articles on both of them as well as a variety of You Tube instructional videos available to you on the internet.

Different social media sites have different uses, strengths and advantages and by using a variety of them it will boost awareness about your business. Twitter is what is called a real time social networking site, a place for sharing information as it happens. It is also for connecting with other people in real time and the results are often a large group of lasting friendships and contacts. Linkedin is a business oriented social networking site where you can build a professional identity on line, discover professional opportunities, business deals and new ventures.

Signing up for a Twitter account is free and it's simple. All you need to do is go to www.twitter.com and fill in the form: your full name, your email address, a username, a password and then type the captcha verification and click sign up and you are done.

Let's talk a little bit about Twitter …. Twitter is an online social networking and microblogging service that enables users to send and read short 140 character message called "tweets". It's an easy way to find out about the latest news related to subjects that interest you and it's a great way to spread the news about your business. Inside a tweet you will see videos, interesting behind the scenes stories about some of the biggest stars and often you will find links to news stories, blogs, websites and apps.

Twitter was developed as a mobile service and the tweets were limited to 140 characters so that it would fit into the character limit of a text message. Twitter is very fast paced because of the brevity of the message, encouraging people to focus on they main idea that they are trying to communicate. Once you tweet, it is publicly posted on your profile; so that people can follow your stream of tweets on what is called a timeline, very similar to Facebook. A person that is interested in your tweets simply has to click on the Follow button next to your name.

In order to find people on Twitter, you can search for their name or Twitter handle or simply import your contacts and Twitter will find these friends for you if they have a Twitter account.

When you set up your Twitter account, you will complete a profile that will tell people what they can expect from your tweets and why they should follow you.

Twitter does have some specific lingo that you will need to learn in order to use the site effectively. These include the symbol @ before a tweet which indicates that you are referring to other users, or a # before a tweet or before a specific word when you are referring to external links. This symbol # as we all know it is called a pound sign, but on Twitter it is called a hastag and it makes certain words easily searchable. The letters "RT" before a tweet means that you have taken a post from another user and retweeted it, automatically crediting the source, so that all your followers can see the tweet. To retweet a post you simply put RT@ (than the username) of the person that originally posted it followed by the contents of the tweet. Your experience on Twitter can just be among some close friends or as   big as you want it to be.

Never underestimate the power of following people that are interesting to you because often times they will follow you back thus creating a larger audience that will see your tweets. One important thing to keep in mind is to keep your tweets interesting and relevant.

I know that it sounds confusing, but trust me once you get into the site and start tweeting you will be a pro in no time. Look at other users tweets and learn from them and you will be on your way to building an unbelievable network.

Now let's talk about Linkedin …. Signing up for a Linkedin account is also free and simple. Just go to www.linkedin.com and fill in the form: first name, last name, email address and password and then click join now and you're done. You will find a variety of profiles from lawyers, accountants, musicians, marketing directors, real estate agents and businesses. Similar to Facebook you have the ability to set up a personal page as well as a business page. To set up a company page enter your name and company email address, then verify that you are eligible to create a page on behalf of the company. Then you create a company profile. Give a description of your company and an overview of what your company does its specialties and what makes your business unique. This is a great place to put that Unique Marketing Statement that we discussed in Chapter #1 Your Marketing Plan. You can also add your company's logo and a banner to bring your page to life.

Promote your company page by connecting with other people that you know who have a profile on the site. Once you start connecting to other users Linkedin will also suggest other similar users that might be interested in your profile. Building a strong network on Linkedin is very easy and does not take long at all. Don't forget to also include the Linkedin button on your website so that people can easily connect to your profile right from your website. One of the other features on Linkedin is the Linkedin

Groups. There are Linkedin groups for almost every industry, profession or skill set. These groups are a great opportunity to make new connections, brag about your expertise, by answering questions that are brought up by the group and to keep your finger on the pulse of what is going on in your particular industry.

There are so many ways to use Twitter and Linkedin to help grow your business and the information that I have given you is just a start. Get on these sites and experiment, click on links, gather information and begin to develop a feel for what other users are doing.

If you stopped reading this book right now and just followed the advice I have given you to this point about your marketing plan, marketing budget, website, Facebook, Twitter and Linkedin you will start to see your business grow to the next level.

I hope by this point in the book you are beginning to understand a little bit about marketing and cross marketing between your website and other social media sites. This is a very important technique that is often over looked by many companies and it is vital to the overall exposure and growth of your business.

Chapter # 7

Branding Your Business

This chapter in my opinion is one of the most important chapters in this book. Branding your business is what customers will remember about your company. For example: when I say facial tissue ... what comes to mind? Most people would say Kleenex. As a matter of fact most people don't even say facial tissue they say I need a box of Kleenex. That is because they did an excellent job of branding. A few other great brands are Volkswagen, Nike, Pepsi, Walmart, Apple, BMW, Canon, Coca Cola, IBM, Lego, MasterCard, Mercedes, Mazda, MGM and Xerox. Do you get the picture?

Pick one of the names I mentioned above .... Can you see the logo in your mind? That's because they did a great job of branding and they did it with a great logo and a great tagline. For example: Walmart has their logo and right underneath the logo it says "Save Money, Live Better" and Nike has their logo and their tagline is "Just Do It"

Here are some other great taglines you might remember: Where's the beef, Got Milk, They melt in your mouth not in your hand and When it absolutely, positively has to be there overnight.

I talked about logos in a previous chapter and I mentioned that you needed to have a logo so people will recognize your business. A good logo will go a long way and unless you are able to create one on your own that looks professional, you will need to hire an expert. You can easily find graphic designers in your area that can help you design a logo without spending a lot of money.

So .... What makes a logo good? There are a few key elements that make a logo successful:

1. It must be functional – It must work on letterhead, business cards, brochures, business signage and vehicle signage as well as on company uniforms.

2. It must be aesthetic – It must be clean and free flowing and it must be readable and understandable.

3. It should be original – If you use stock art or clip art it is going to show, original art always works best.

4. It has to be appropriate – It needs to have something to do with your business. If you are a painter incorporate something to do with painting like a brush or a roller. Using a large diamond surrounded by the name of your company wouldn't fit your image.

5. Keep it simple – A complex drawing with an obscure design will confuse potential customers. Keep the drawing clean and simple.

The next thing you want to work on is a good catch phrase like Walmart and Nike. One of the companies that I work with is a pest control company and he treats his customers properties with "green" natural chemicals instead of the toxic chemicals used by their competitors and his catch phrase is "Protecting Families, Businesses and the Environment" this coupled with his very simple logo that clearly depicts the name of his company with a few green leaves has worked wonders for growing his company.

Now that you have your logo, what should you do with it? The answer is simple put it everywhere and I mean everywhere. This logo should be on your business cards, letterheads, estimates, invoices, brochures or any printed material that your company uses. It should also be on your website, your Facebook page, your Twitter page, your company signage on your office or store and most importantly on your vehicles. I also suggest to all my clients that they should have company uniforms for all their employees and the logo should be either screen printed or embroidered on them. I prefer embroidery, because it looks more crisp and professional. One of my customers that own a restaurant has all his wait staff, bus boys and delivery drivers in polo shirts with the logo on it and his cooks have chefs' jackets with the logo. Another company that I work with has all its sales reps in polo shirts in the warm weather and in dress shirts in the colder weather with the logo on it. My friend that has the pest control company has all of his technicians in polo shirts and in the colder months he supplies them with a very nice three season jacket with the company logo. It is simple and clean and it makes a great appearance when they are dealing with customers. Many of my customers use a company by the name of Queensboro, which has a variety of apparel for any type of business. I am told that they have great deals and they even run specials throughout the year. I suggest you check out their website at www.queensboro.com or check with a local screen printing and embroidery company in your area.

Chapter 8

Free Ads On Backpage and Craigslist

Let's talk for a few minutes about "FREE" ads for your business on Backpage and Craigslist. These two sites are a great place to advertise your business and if you have never tried it … you are missing out.

I have several clients that use both of these sites on a regular basis with great results and doesn't cost a thing if you do it right.

So let's get started …. simply go to www.backpage.com or www.craigslist.com and then choose the area that you want to advertise in. It is important to note that they will only let you run an ad in one location at a time for free. If you try to do multiple locations there is a slight fee. You can however get around paying the fee by waiting an hour or two between posts and slightly changing the content of your post.

When you get to the main page of the area you want to advertise in, you will see a number of headings and under each heading there are a number of categories. Find the category that best fits your business and click on it. For example under the heading "Services" you will find categories like: Biz Opps, Business, Cleaning, Computer, Creative, Financial, Health & Beauty, Home Improvement, Landscape/Lawn, Labor/Moving, Legal, Massage, Misc, and Real Estate.

I suggest that you click on a few of them and see what type of ads other people have placed so you can get some ideas about placing your ad.

Let's use Home Improvement as an example. When you click on it another page will open showing headlines of various ads and they are broken down by the date in which the ads were placed.

If you click on the headline of the ad another page will open taking you to that ad. As you can see the headline needs to be catchy so it will attract a customer who is searching for your type of service.

To place an ad all you have to do is click on the button at the top of the page that says "Post an Ad". Once you click on that button and information page will open and it is very self explanatory … All you need to do is fill in all the required information and then at the bottom click on the submit button. Before your ad can be published they will send you an email with a link to the ad so you can see how it will look when it goes live on their site. In the email you will have the opportunity to edit your ad or confirm your email address and place the ad.

Here are a few suggestions for designing your ad:

1.   Make your headline short but catchy and do not write it in all caps. Keep your headline clean and to the point.

2.   Make sure the body of the ad gives great descriptions of what you do or what you are trying to sell and be honest … people know scam artists when they see one. Don't be afraid to give a lot of detail … there is no word limit on these sites. Make sure your spelling is correct. Copy and paste the ad to Microsoft word and spell check the ad if you are not sure.

3.   Make sure you give the person in the ad a few ways to get in touch with you (email, phone, website etc.)

4.   Use good, clear pictures…important note: most people don't click on ads that don't have pictures. So use pictures if you want to get some activity.

If you are pretty computer savvy there are a number of videos on You Tube that can show you how to design and post an HTML type ad to these sites. I am not going to get into that in this book, because it is pretty involved and would take up a lot of pages to explain. The videos on You Tube are great and they take you step by step with on screen pictures and tips. So if you're interested in taking your ads to the next level simply do a google search for Craigslist or Backpage picture ads or HTML ads and you will find plenty of information that will guide you through the process.

Chapter # 9

Email Marketing

newsletters, special promotions, coupons &

new product announcements

Email marketing is a very effective way to get the word out to your current customers and prospective customers that have subscribed to you email list.

Let's start with your email list …. you do have one …. don't you? If you don't then … now is the time to start compiling one, because every business regardless of what product you sell or what service you provide you should have a customer database that contains your customer's information (name, address, telephone number and email address, as well as birthdays & anniversaries).

Once you have an email list use it to send out monthly newsletters, information about special promotions, coupons for your customers' birthdays, anniversary or even customer loyalty. You can also send out emails to announce any new products or services. It's easy to do and it's free.

There are a few ways that you can put this information together and send it to your customer list. One way is to design it using an art program and saving the file to a PDF format and then attach it to an email and the other way is to set up an account with a company like Constant Contact who you can find at www.constantcontact.com

Constant Contact has a variety of different templates that are easy to use and that have great flexibility. Check them out and take advantage of their free 30 day trial before you sign-up for any of their programs. The cost of using Constant Contact is minimal and depends on how many customers you will be uploading to your database. The last time I looked it was $15.00 a month for up to 500 stored email addresses and $30.00 a month for 500-2500. I have personally been using Constant Contact for my email marketing campaigns for about 5 years now and it is the easiest way to reach your customer base that I have found. Constant Contact also gives you a variety of things that you can use to boost your email list, so make sure you take a look at their business building tips.

Email marketing should be used to reach your customer database and make them aware of upcoming sales or any special promotions. It is also a great way to introduce new products to the customers that already buy from you or to reward these customers with a special coupon for their next visit. You can even design monthly or quarterly newsletters and let your customers know about what is going on in your industry.

Email marketing is a MUST in your marketing mix and is a very effective way to keep in touch with the customers you already have a relationship with. Use it a few times a year and you will be surprised and how much revenue it will generate for your business.

Chapter 10

Radio & Television Advertising

Do not skip this chapter … because you are thinking … I don't have a big enough budget to advertise on the radio or the television!

The truth of the matter is …. you don't have to spend a fortune on these two excellent advertising vehicles. Let me give you an example: One of my customers who owns a medical supply company wanted to advertise on the radio, but he kept putting it off because he thought it would be too expensive. During one of our marketing sessions I brought up the topic of radio and he said I thought about it but I don't have that type of budget. So I asked him how much he thought it would be and his answer was "I don't really know because I never looked into it" … "I just assumed it would be very expensive". Does that sound like you?

We reviewed his marketing plan and we talked for awhile about who his target market really is and then we discussed the radio stations in the area and did some research to find out which station would best reach his target market. We then contacted the station and set-up a meeting with the sales rep for his area. The sales rep provided us with all the demographic information about the station, the average age of the listeners, their income, sex, ethnic background etc. During this conversation we discovered that this station had a Sunday Morning talk show that aired every Sunday for one hour and that the people that listened to that talk show were exactly the people my client wanted to reach. We then found out that there just so happened to be one advertising spot open on that show and for a 1 minute commercial it was only $125.00. The sales rep told my client that because of the popularity of that show that they were looking for a 4 week commitment. So for $500.00

he got 1 commercial a week for four weeks on a show that was geared right at his target market group. He signed the contract and after the first Sunday the commercial aired his phone rang like crazy on Monday morning from people that didn't even know that his business was right there in their neighborhood. His sales that week more than paid for what he had paid for the 4 commercials and he still had three weeks to go.

It goes back to what I said earlier in the book …. Find Out Who Your Target Market Is …. And Advertise To Them!

So do your homework and be clear of who your target market is and then talk to the Radio & TV sales reps that handle your area. Another one of my customers who owned a garden center, had a TV commercial produced that he ran on HGTV once a week on a show that was specifically targeted to people sprucing up their homes and yards. After about three weeks of running that ad, his garden center was packed. Now do you think that ad would have done that well if he had aired it on the sci-fi channel … maybe, but very unlikely to say the least.

Another thing you need to know about Radio & TV is that there are always specials going on, news & weather sponsorships, or an event that the station is running like an Easter egg hunt at the county park. These types of sponsorships are usually sold in a package deal format and they give you a bunch of 1 minute commercials, plus a number of on air mentions every time the radio station talks about the event. In addition, you usually get your company logo on the stations website. If the event is something that your target market would be interested in … than this also would be a great opportunity to get your name out there.

The other opportunities that arise when you have a relationship with a Radio or Television station is un-sold time slots … these are usually sold at great bargains, because they need to fill up these time slots … so evaluate when the spots would air and see if it fits into the habits of your target market and if it does … sometimes you can grab a bunch of these ads at half or a third of what the normal cost would have been. You will however only know about these spots if you have a working relationship with the sales rep and they have a commercial on file for your business that can easily be popped into that time slot.

So don't shy away from Radio & Television ads. Look into the stations in your area, gather your information and talk to a few sales reps about what they have to offer. Let them know who your target market is and ask if they have any specific programs that fit that market. Also let them know that you would be open to special promotions and un-sold time slots that would reach your market and you're on your way.

Chapter # 11

Direct Mail Advertising

Direct Mail advertising is anything that is mailed directly to the customer. The most common are postcards, brochures, catalogs and coupons. These types of mailings in most cases can be pinpointed to a specific target market group or a specific neighborhood zip code. Direct mail advertising returns are usually anywhere between .5% and 1.5% depending on how good your offer is.

I am not going to spend a lot of time on this because I know when I get direct mail pieces sent to my home or office I usually put it right in the garbage. When I get those envelopes filled with coupons, I usually browse through them very quickly and pull out the one or two that I think I might use and the rest go in the trash. The return rates are low and with the cost of printing and postage today the cost far out weighs the return on investment in my opinion.

If you decide to try a direct mail campaign I can only give you the following advice:

1.   Make sure the piece your mailing is eye-catching, and in full color so that maybe the customer will look at it.

2.   Make sure its going to reach your target market.

3.   Tell an interesting story and get to the point.

4.   Make sure it's a great offer.

5.   Make sure the piece doesn't look cheap or like it was designed by a 3rd grader.

6. Be patient, you might not get an immediate response; some people might tack it to their refrigerator or put on their desk for when the time is right.

7. Make sure you track your response against what it cost you and what type of revenue it generated.

8. If you are offering a discount use dollar amounts rather than percentages ($10.00 off instead of 15% off). Dollar amounts outperform percentage off offers almost three to one.

Now that I said all of that, let me tell you about the direct mail marketing that have a higher return rate. If you are mailing postcards, brochures, coupons or catalogs to your existing customer base the rate of return jumps to a 10%-20% return rate. This however depends upon how recently the customers you are mailing to have purchased from you or utilized your services.

There are a lot of companies on the internet that offer services for direct mail marketing, so if you decide to utilize this method do your research and compare their rates for designing and mailing your campaign.

Chapter #12

Print Advertising

In this chapter I am going to talk about newspapers, placemats, billboards, fax blasts, door hangers, lawn signs, brochures, community & school ad journals, church and synagogue newsletters and bulletins as well as press releases and business profiles.

Let's start with newspapers …. I know that the amount of newspapers have dwindled over the past few years because of the internet, but there are still quite a few of them out there depending on where you live and yes … there are a lot of people that still like to read them. Newspaper advertising can be very effective and it is a great part of any marketing mix. Let me give you an example, my friend that owned the medical supply store found a newspaper that was delivered to the homes in a 55+ adult community. This was perfect for his business, because his target market was people 55+ years old who needed his products (knee braces, back braces, wheelchairs, canes, walkers etc). Now I am not saying that everybody that is 55+ needs his products, but that age group also has parents that might need them, so they are a good part of his target market. These 55+ communities usually publish their newspapers once a month and it contains all the events going on in the community as well as results of the bocce ball tournaments and information about when certain groups or organizations meet. This is why this paper gets read by the residents of the community and why his return on investment is so good. So once again, find a newspaper that reaches your target market. It is also important to note that much like radio and television … newspapers often have what are called "remnant" space. This is unsold advertising space that they need to fill before they go to print. If you have a good working relationship with your salesperson he or she will probably call you and ask you if you want to take advantage of this unsold space. These remnants usually sell for far less than the cost of a regular ad and most times they need your answer on the spot so that they can finish the paper and go to print.

I know that I sound repetitious but this is the key to an effective marketing campaign. Having spent 25+ years in this business you can not believe the numbers of businesses that I have come across that don't know why they are advertising in the places that they are running their ads and they have no idea of what their return on investment is. This is shocking to me that businesses would just advertise for the sake of advertising and not track their return on the investment. So if this book saves you time and money and helps you grow your business … then I accomplished what I was trying to do.

Placemat advertising in your local diner or restaurant …. it's cheap and yes it does work, because while people are waiting for their food they read the placemats. Now don't go crazy and advertise on every placemat in your town. Find a restaurant or a diner (if you have those where you live) that is frequented by the people that fit your target market and try it for a few months. I had a friend that ran an ad on a diner placemat that said bring this ad in and receive a free gift and he got over 100 coupons within a two week period. The manager at the diner said that when many people were done eating they would ask their waitress for another copy of placemat to take home so that they would have a clean copy to cut out the ads.

The same thing goes for community and school ad journals as well as church and synagogue newsletters and bulletins. People like to patronize businesses that support their community events, schools and religious organizations. Like I said before don't run ads in every one of them but try out one or two here and there and see what kind of results you get. For the most part these are also very inexpensive and in most cases you can run an ad as small as a business card.

Billboards … yes they work, but only if they are strategically located to where your business is located because you are trying to attract people to stop by right then and there when they see the billboard. This can be very expensive and require long contracts so make sure you do your homework.

Fax Blasts … these can very annoying to customers or potential customers if you do it to often so be careful how you utilize this method. A friend of mine that owns a breakfast and lunch cafe gets great results from using the fax blast by sending out the specials for that day and offering free delivery to those businesses in the area. As a result … he tripled his lunch business in one week.

Brochures … are a great way to tell a story about your company and a very important marketing tool for your business. If you don't have a brochure you can easily put one together on the Vistaprint website www.vistaprint.com they have great templates for almost every business that allows you to add pictures as well as text and most of them are in full color and they look very professional. I have used this site many times and designed brochures for a number of my clients. Your brochure should tell a story about your business and contain all the information that you want a prospective customer to know about your business. Gather up some brochures from other businesses especially your competitors before you start to design yours and get a feel for what other companies have included in their brochure and than make yours even better.

Door Hangers and Lawn Signs …. are two great ways to promote your business especially if you are in a business such as landscaping, painting, pest control, power washing etc. If you are in one of these businesses or something similar …door hangers and lawn signs are a must. When you are doing a job at a house make sure you put your lawn sign right out front near the street, so the neighbors can see it. Then have one of your employees go around to every home on that block and put a door hanger on their door knobs. Sounds simple doesn't it? Yes it is, but most people in these types of businesses overlook this easy marketing technique. One of my clients used this simple technique and said that by using the lawn signs and door hangers he would get at least 1 or 2 more jobs in that neighborhood every time he did it. He said that before he used this technique he rarely got work from any of the neighbors.

Keep your lawn signs simple, all you need is the company name and a phone number. A great place to get quick inexpensive double sided lawn signs without ordering large quantities is a company called Signs on the Cheap and you can find them at www.signsonthecheap.com

Door Hangers should say something like: We are working at your neighbor's house at (blank) or we just finished a job at your neighbor's house at (blank) and it should contain information about your services and of course your company name and a phone number. One of my clients uses them with his landscape business with great results. All he does is fill in the blank with the address of the house he was working on and then slip them onto all the doorknobs in the area. You can find great door hangers at www.labelsonthefly.com or www.doorhangers.com both of these sites have great prices and great turnaround times. Many local printers can also provide these, so shop around your area.

Press Releases and Business Profiles are also another great way to get your company name out there. Press Releases are simple, just write it and send it to your local newspaper and if it's interesting most papers will find room for them. Press Releases can be as simple as your company hired a new person, or is announcing a new product or service. Not every press release that you write and submit is going to make it into a publication but be consistent and keep sending them in. One of my clients who owned a vitamin and health food store took my advice and after about two months of writing and sending in press releases he received a call from the editor of the paper who told him that he loves his press releases and wanted to know if he would be interested in writing a weekly column for the paper. My client of course agreed and his column ran in that newspaper for three years and it was all free advertising for his business. Make sure that you update your media contact list on a regular basis because editors at these publications change quite often.

Business Profiles are fantastic and will attract a lot of prospective customers to your business. To get a business profile in a newspaper or magazine you must first have some history with advertising in that publication. Once you have that relationship, simply call the editor and ask if they ever feature a business in their publication and you will find that most of them do that on a regular basis. The business profile is great because it's a story about your business complete with pictures and it's usually a half or full page feature. Best of all most publications do not charge for this service and it is a great form of free advertising.

Chapter #13

Networking Events

Networking events can be a variety of different things. It can be an organized meeting of professionals or business owners that meet for breakfast, lunch or dinner to swap business leads and referrals. It can be a business card exchange where business people get together and swap business cards and get to know each other. It can be as simple as a cigar dinner sponsored by a local restaurant or a golf luncheon sponsored by the local golf course. Whatever the event … it's a great opportunity to meet other business people, share stories and build relationships. The beauty of it is you never know who you might meet that someday could be a great referral source for your business and vice versa.

Do some research and I am sure that you will find a number of networking events in your area to attend. One of the local country clubs in my area holds a networking cocktail party once a quarter and all you need to attend is to pay a nominal fee usually about from $25 per person and a stack of business cards. When you register they give you a name badge that has your first name and company name on it and you just walk around and talk to the other people in the room. I know exactly what your thinking … I can't do that, just walk around and talk to people I don't even know. Well my friend, it is time to step out of your comfort zone and put on your big boy pants and get out and make some new contacts. You can't do that sitting in your office hiding behind your desk.

When most people think about networking it seems insincere at best and selfish at worst … when it is supposed to be friendly, useful and genuine. Your goal in networking should be to help other people, because networking is a two way street. Make sure that you understand the other persons needs before you tell them about yours. You don't need to know the most people at the event … just the right people. Don't ever expect anything, because some of the people you meet will respond and some won't. Don't leave networking to chance … have a good idea of the types of people that you want to meet. Find people that are somehow related to your industry who you can share leads and contacts with. Don't ever dismiss anyone as irrelevant, because you never know who that person might be able to introduce you too. After you meet people at an event, follow up with them by email, but keep your emails short and to the point.

Make networking a habit. Try to contact at least one new person a day. This means if you reach out to 5 new people a week you would have contacted 250 people a year. Remember that not everyone is going to get back to you, but if you contact that many people, then you are bound to make some great contacts. I have collected so many business cards and have made so many contacts over the years, that no matter what somebody is looking for I probably know somebody that can help them and many of my friends and clients call me on a regular basis when they are looking for somebody and all most all of the time I can say … Yes I know just the person you should contact. My contact list consists of doctors, attorneys, accountants, newspaper editors, graphic artists, sign companies, printers, all types of home improvement contractors, appraisers, physical therapists, caterers and I could go on and on … but I think you get the picture. Build your network, share leads, refer to people you know and you will get referrals in return.

Chapter # 14

Video Marketing

Video marketing is a new type of internet marketing in which businesses create a 2-5 minute video about a specific topic and then upload the video to various video sharing websites like You Tube. These videos can then also be shared via email by sending people the link to your video as well as uploading the videos to your website and other social media platforms.

First let's talk about You Tube. You Tube is an online public communications site that allows registered users to upload their videos and make them public, so that they can be viewed by anyone.

Ok … so why should I use it? Wells that's easy. No matter what type of video that you want to watch or post, you can do it all on You Tube. When you own a business, it is a great tool for getting your product out there for little or no cost. It's a great way to run ongoing information about new products or services to the same people or new people.

The first thing you need to do is set up your account on You Tube at www.youtube.com. Once you go to the site all you need to do is follow the instructions and set up your free account. It's that simple!

You Tube has a built in photo slideshow or video upload editing device that is easy use. Just sign into your account and then click on Upload… the next window will give you a few options either webcam capture, photo slide show, Google+ hangout and also video editor.

For the purposes of this example we are going to use the easiest option, which is photo slide show. Click on the create button under the photo slideshow and this will take you to the next page which will allow you to upload pictures that are on your computer or in your Google album. Simply click on the pictures you want and upload them. Once you have the pictures uploaded you can then click on them and move them around to the order that you want. The next step will let you add background music from about 150,000 default soundtracks. You can also go into advanced editor which will let you choose video effects and let you add text on to the photos or even create a text page with your company name and information.

Once you're done all you need to do is click upload and it will begin to set up your video slide show for publication. While it is preparing your video, make sure you fill in all the information on the screen: the video title, description, tags, and your category. There are also a number of other ways to upload more sophisticated videos using Microsoft power point or more advanced video editing software that are available on the internet.

Once you have your first video uploaded then you want to share that video on your website, Facebook and other social media and attract customers to view it.

There are plenty of "How To" videos and articles on publishing videos to You Tube for more advanced users which are great once you become more comfortable.

Chapter 15

Internal Marketing

Internal marketing is something that should be done on an on going basis within your company. Some great internal marketing techniques are: an open house, customer referral programs, special events & contests, gift certificates, customer satisfaction surveys, good customer relations and thank you cards or notes.

Depending on the type of business that you own you might be able to utilize all or just a few of these so pick the techniques that are best suited for your business.

If you have the type of business where customers come to you then having an open house or a customer appreciation day where you can invite people into your business works great. You can do things like meet the staff and give tours of your business. Make sure that you have some refreshments and that you hand out advertising specialties like pens, calendars, post-it notes etc. with you company logo and message.

Customer referral programs are a great way to get new customers from your existing customer base with little or no cost. Simply ask your customers, who they might know that would be interested in your products or services and give them something in return for their referral. I have clients that have offered a Visa gift card, a coupon toward their next purchase or a gift certificate for dinner at a local restaurant. This is a great way to get new customers and retain existing customers and it costs very little in comparison to a major advertising campaign.

Sending out thank you cards or a thank you note by mail or email to a customer for using your company is also another great way to show customers you care and you appreciate their business.

Gift certificates are also a great internal marketing tool if it is suitable to your particular business. Gift certificates are a great way for your existing customers to tell their friends about your business and give them their first experience with your company.

Customer satisfaction surveys are a great tool to see what kind of a job you are doing and to help you in refining your marketing plan to meet the needs of your target market.

Great customer relations in any business is the most important key to the success and the growth of your business. Make sure that everybody on your staff is well trained in answering the phones, handling customer problems, collecting money, follow-up & answering customer inquiries. These staff members are the first line of communication with your customers and they can easily make or break the deal. Let me give you an example: I was having knee problems and I was looking for an orthopedic surgeon to go to for a consult and a friend of mine recommended a very experienced surgeon that was on top of all the modern procedures and probably one of the best in his field. I called the office and the person who answered the phone was very arrogant and nasty almost as if I was bothering her with my questions. Needless to say I did not make an appointment with that surgeon and I had to wonder how many other people did the same thing. About a week later I saw an advertisement for another surgeon who was also very experienced and had the credentials to also be one of the best in his field. I called his office and the person answering the phone was happy, upbeat and honestly sounded as if she was interested in helping me. She transferred me to another person who was equally as nice and as a result I scheduled an appointment. Dealing with this physician's office over the next several months I found that everybody in that surgeon's office had great customer service skills and they truly were more than happy to answer my questions and help me in any way that they could.

When somebody calls your business … is your staff winning customers or losing them?

I know everybody has a bad day now and then and that people have problems in their personal lives, whether it be financial problems, their kids, their spouse or even sickness. That being said … they need to leave their problems at the door when they get to work … or get them off the phones and away from dealing with your customers!

Chapter 16

There Is More

I hope that by this point in the book that I have given you some techniques that you can use to grow your business, but there is more. In this chapter I want to briefly give you some additional ideas that work and that can easily be implemented in your business.

1. Speaking at local groups and organizations – search out groups and organizations in your area and contact them and let them know that you are available to speak to their organization. Most groups that meet regularly are always looking for programs at their meetings.

2. Sponsor local events – I am sure that there are a number of events happening in your area that would welcome your sponsorship. These include but are not limited to golf outing fund raisers, charity fund-raising walks and school plays. Your local scout troops, fire departments, baseball teams, soccer teams, first aid squads, cancer support groups, autism groups and the list goes on. Most if not all of these are always looking for companies to sponsor their events and this is a great way to give back to the community and get your name out in front of hundreds or even thousands of people.

3. Chamber of Commerce Events – if you are not a member of your local chamber of commerce … then join today. Your chamber is a great way to meet other business people in your area and network.

4. Local web based directories – if you did a good job with your website you should already be listed in a variety search engine directories but there are more. Spend some time surfing the web

and look for local directories where you can add your business name and information about your company. The best part is that many of them are free and after filling out a brief questionnaire they will gladly add your business to their list.

5. Marketing with non-competitive business neighbors – find other businesses in your area that have similar target markets as you business and market with them. This could be as simple as putting your company literature in their business so that they can share it with their customers. In turn you can do the same for them at your business.

6. Fraternal Organizations – get involved in organizations in your area like Rotary, Lions, Elks, or the Knights of Columbus. Not only can these organizations use your expertise but it's a great way to give back to your community and make some great contacts.

7. Cold Calling / Face To Face Interaction – yes sometimes we need to get back to our roots and get out there and meet prospective customers just like we did when we first started our business. Nothing takes the place of face to face interaction with prospective customers!

8. Trade shows, health fairs and expos – these events are a great way to showcase your business and get your name out to prospective customers. Make sure that you have company branded give-a-way items to give out so that people remember who you are and what you do. Another great promotion at these events is to have a special promotion and or contest at your booth. Offer special show pricing to anybody that visits your booth, have a drawing at your booth so that prospective customers have to fill out an entry form. Make sure the entry form contains pertinent information like a phone number and email address so that you can add these people to your marketing campaigns and follow-up with them after the show.

Do you have enough ideas yet? Are there techniques in this book that you are not using? What techniques can you implement in your business tomorrow?

In the words of Nike " just do it" … you are now armed with proven techniques that will grow your business, but none of them will work if you just take this book and put it on the shelf and forget about them. Use this book as reference guide and make sure that your business is making use of as many techniques as you can.

Remember what I said earlier in the book … "Make sure that you actively engage in at least one marketing activity every day".

Chapter 17

Summary

I have given you a lot of information in this book and I know that if you take my advice and use these techniques that you will have no problem growing your business.

Let's just take a few minutes and summarize some of the important points that we covered in this book:

1. Develop a marketing plan.

2. Establish a marketing budget.

3. Make sure that you have a company website and make sure that it is mobile-optimized.

4. Get a Business Facebook page.

5. Register with Linkedin and Twitter.

6. Cross market all of your social media sites.

7. Make sure that you have a good logo and you begin to brand your business.

8. Develop an email customer database.

9. Attend networking events as often as possible.

10. Take advantage of any free advertising that you can like Backpage, Craigslist, News Releases & Business Profiles.

11. Utilize different forms of print advertising.

12. Look into Radio and TV advertising.

13. Don't forget about video marketing on You Tube and share those videos across all of your social media sites.

14. Maintain good internal   marketing procedures.

15. Speak at local groups and organizations.

16. Sponsor local events.

17. Join the Chamber of Commerce.

18. Market with local non-competitive businesses.

19. Get involved in the community by joining groups like the Rotary, Lions or Elks club.

20. Make sure you are listed correctly in web based directories.

21. Get back to the basics and get out in front of prospective customers.

22. Be persistent in all your efforts and always analyze your returns.

No single marketing technique works all the time for every business, so always rotate several marketing techniques and vary your approach. Customers sometimes tune out after awhile if you constantly use the same tactics.

Remember to revisit your marketing plan and your marketing budget at least once a quarter and make changes as necessary.

Send us your feedback and success stories to: leobusinesssolutions@gmail.com

Chapter 18

Recommended Reading

The books below are great books that every business owner should read. If you have no time to read then find the audio book version and listen to them in your car.

Each one of these books was written by people who are very successful and you will find them very inspiring as you work daily to grow your business.

1. Think Big & Kick Ass by Donald Trump

2. How Come That Idiots Rich & I'm Not by Robert Shemin

3. The E Myth Revisited by Michael Gerber

4. Think & Grow Rich by Napoleon Hill

5. Everyday A Friday by Joel Osteen

6. Effective Networking by David Nour

7. Your Best Life Now by Joel Osteen

8. Think & Grow Rich The Lost Secret by Vic Johnson

About The Author

Joe Leo is the President of Leo Business Solutions, a full service business management and marketing consulting group.

Joe has a degree in Business / Marketing and he has been working in the marketing field for the past 25+ years.

Joe has worked with a number of small and medium sized businesses as well as for some large fortune 500 corporations. In addition he has owned several small businesses that he started, grew and then sold.

His passion for developing marketing programs has catapulted a variety of businesses from the start-up stages to profitable in a short period of time.

Joe is available for speaking engagements, seminars and consulting for any type of business. Joe can also help you with putting together your marketing plan, establishing your marketing budget, graphic design, planning special events, social media and training your staff.

You can reach Joe at leobusinessolutions@gmail.com.